THE ROMANS

Peter Hicks

Thomson Learning

New York

Look into the Past

The Anglo-Saxons
The Aztecs
The Egyptians
The Greeks
The Romans
The Vikings

First published in the
United States in 1994 by
Thomson Learning
115 Fifth Avenue
New York, NY 10003

First published in 1993
by Wayland (Publishers) Ltd.

Library of Congress Cataloging-in-Publication Data
Hicks, Peter, 1952–
  The Romans / Peter Hicks.
    p.   cm. (Look into the past)
  Includes bibliographical references and index.
  Summary: Illustrates the culture and history of ancient
Rome.
  ISBN 1-56847-063-0 : $14.95
  1. Rome – Civilization – Juvenile literature. 2. Rome –
Antiquities – Juvenile literature 3. Romans – Social life and
customs – Juvenile literature. [1. Rome – Civilization.
2. Rome – Antiquities. 3. Rome – Social life and customs.]
I. Title. II. Series.
DG78.H53   1994   93-11653
937-dc20

Printed in Italy

Picture acknowledgments
The publishers wish to thank the following for supplying the
photographs for this book: Canterbury Heritage Museum 29
(top); C. M. Dixon 5 (top), 7 (bottom), 8 (both), 9 (top), 11
(bottom), 12, 13 (right), 17 (top), 18, 19 (bottom), 20, 21
(all), 23 (both), 25 (both), 26 (top); English Heritage 19
(top); Focal Point 9 (bottom), 10, 11 (top), 16, 24; Sonia
Halliday 29 (bottom); Robert Harding 6, 14, 15 (top), 17
(bottom), 22; Peter Hicks 13 (bottom left), 15 (bottom), 27;
The Mansell Collection 28; Wayland 4; Werner Forman
Archive 26 (bottom).
Map artwork by Jenny Hughes.

CONTENTS

Words that appear in **_bold italic_** in the text are explained in the glossary on page 30.

WHO WERE THE ROMANS?

The story of Rome, its people, and the *empire* they built is both impressive and exciting. From a city built on the banks of the Tiber River in central Italy sprang a mighty empire that stretched into three continents and lasted nearly 700 years. The Romans built lasting roads, bridges, and towns. They produced great literature and art, strong government, and a powerful army and navy. However, Roman rule could be very cruel. The Roman army fought many battles and conquered huge areas. They often treated prisoners of war and *civilians* very badly. Also, the whole Roman way of life was based on *slavery*: millions of *slaves* did most of the work. Many slaves led lives of misery.

▼ The founding of Rome is wrapped up in *legend*. It is said that two young brothers, Romulus and Remus, were abandoned on the banks of the Tiber River. A she-wolf appeared from the forest and suckled them, saving them from starvation. The statue here shows this famous event. The wolf is nursing the baby brothers. The legend tells us that they were brought up by a shepherd and his kind wife. According to the legend, Romulus founded Rome in 753 B.C. with the help of the gods. He plowed a trench in the shape of the new city, but then killed his brother Remus in a fight for the throne. The story was perhaps a way of telling the Romans that they were special.

Archaeologists ▶
have discovered that nearly 4,000 years ago a tribe called the Latini were settled and farming in the region where Rome was built. The land was very *fertile* and the weather was good, so crops grew well. Farmers grew grain and vegetables and raised animals. The picture shows a plowman with his team of oxen. The Latini were simple people living in thatched huts. It is believed their small farms gradually developed into villages and towns. The Roman language is called "Latin" because it developed from the language of the Latini.

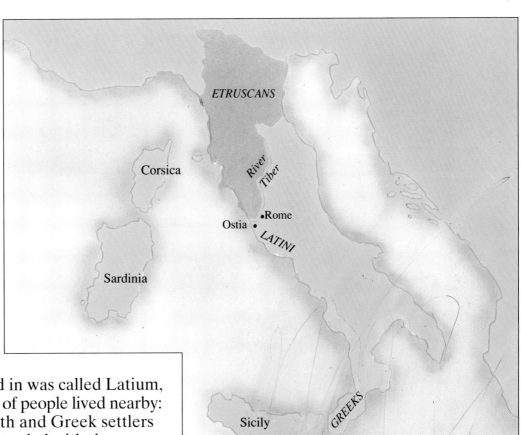

The area the Latini lived in was called Latium, and two powerful groups of people lived nearby: the Etruscans to the north and Greek settlers to the south. The Latini traded with these people, so it is not surprising that they picked up many ideas from them, including ideas about religion and the use of the alphabet. In fact, many of the ideas that made the Roman Empire so great came from the Etruscans and Greeks.

THE GROWTH OF AN EMPIRE

The cluster of tribal settlements that came together to form the city of Rome was situated on a group of hills above the Tiber River. The high ground and the river protected Rome from enemy attack. The city was also 15 miles upstream from the Mediterranean Sea, which meant it was unlikely to be attacked by pirates roaming the Mediterranean. But it was not too far from the sea for Roman traders to reach the sea routes. Below the hills, the Tiber narrows, making an excellent bridging point for travelers and traders. It is not surprising that, in such a good position, Rome grew quickly.

▲ One problem Rome faced was lowland flooding near the Tiber. Once this area was successfully drained, it was made into an open space for meetings called the forum, the remains of which you can see in the picture. The city council met in a building called the curia at the forum. People also went to the forum to trade goods and to listen to speeches.

Rome had to deal with several attacks by her neighbors before becoming a strong empire. But by 146 B.C. Rome controlled all the trade in the Mediterranean and felt strong enough to expand. The Roman army conquered the Greeks to the east and moved north and west.

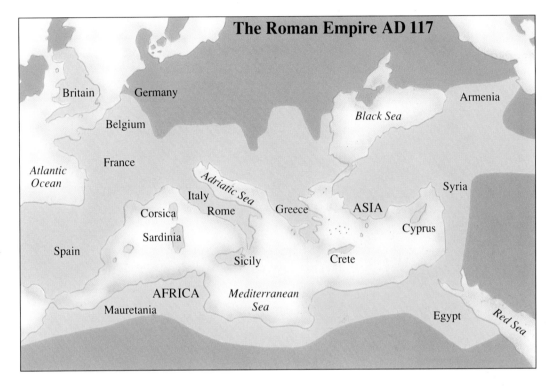

The Roman Empire AD 117

Britain
Germany
Belgium
France
Atlantic Ocean
Italy
Rome
Corsica
Sardinia
Spain
Sicily
AFRICA
Mauretania
Mediterranean Sea
Adriatic Sea
Greece
Black Sea
Armenia
ASIA
Syria
Cyprus
Crete
Egypt
Red Sea

◀ This map of the Roman Empire shows the land that Rome conquered. Every time they defeated a tribe, the Romans set up a province. When a new province was brought into the empire, all its wealth and goods were taken. These would be grain, animals, and wine; money through taxes; valuable metals such as iron, lead, or gold; and human beings to be sold as slaves.

The carvings on this column in Rome ▶ show the Roman army capturing a **barbarian** village. It is a shocking scene – men are being killed, homes are being destroyed, as an old man prays to his gods for help. A woman and child try to escape, but a soldier pulls the woman back by the hair. The villagers will be taken prisoner and sold as slaves. After a war, slaves were plentiful and cheap, and many rich Romans bought them. Some masters took good care their slaves, but many slaves were treated cruelly and **branded** like animals on the forehead or leg, as the property of their owners.

By A.D. 100, with all the wealth pouring into Rome from the Empire, the city was the largest and most impressive in the world. A million people lived there. The model of Rome gives us a good idea of what the city looked like.

As the model shows, the city was crowded with houses, apartments, public baths, and shops. The huge Colosseum stands on the right and the Circus Maximus is in the foreground. These buildings were where the Roman Games took place.

◀ Huge amounts of grain were needed for the large population and Rome, therefore, depended on receiving plentiful amounts from the Empire. Free grain was given out to the poor and, if this ran out, riots would often take place. This *mosaic* shows a man measuring corn, a vital crop for the Romans.

By A.D. 100 the ▶
Roman Empire was a
huge area with an
emperor at its head.
The Empire was
linked by an
impressive network of
roads. Many Roman
roads were long and
straight. Straight
roads allowed troops
to travel quickly and
directly to any trouble
spots in the Empire.
Many of these straight
roads built by the
Romans still exist
today.

◀ The Romans also
built roads to cross
mountains. Here a
road leads twisting
and turning over the
Alps. This was built
by the Romans and
shows what excellent
engineers they were.

THE ARMY

The Roman Empire would never have grown had it not been for the efficient army. We know a lot about the army, because its troops went to many places and left behind a lot of evidence of their presence. The Roman army was divided into huge groups called legions. A legion could contain up to 6,000 soldiers. In the early days of the Roman Empire, soldiers were part-timers, which meant they were called only when they were needed to fight. As the size of the Empire increased the soldiers were employed full-time. When men joined the army they had to stay for twenty-five years.

The best trained, ▶ best equipped, and highest paid Roman soldier was the legionary. The only people who could become legionaries were Roman *citizens* or the sons of legionaries. In the picture, a small group of them is shown wearing helmets and carrying spears and rectangular shields. The shields were used to attack as well as to defend. Legionaries not only had to fight, but were also expected to be good builders and engineers. When not fighting, they were expected to build camps, forts, roads, bridges, and walls.

◀ Here is one example of the evidence left behind by Roman soldiers. When the army attacked Maiden Castle in England in A.D. 43, they shot one of the defenders with a ballista bolt – a heavy arrow shot from a crossbow. When the site was *excavated* by archaeologists they found his body, with the iron tip of the arrow still in one of the bones in his spine.

▼ This picture shows a section from Trajan's Column, in Rome, which tells the story of the war against a tribe called the Dacians. The legionaries are hard at work constructing a fort. Ditches are being dug, and fort walls and wooden fences are being built.

▼ The two soldiers on guard with the round shields were called auxiliaries. They were recruited into the army from the tribes conquered by the Romans. By doing this, the Romans passed their customs on to people in the areas that were conquered. The main job of the auxiliaries was to support the legions in battle. In fact, auxiliaries were often sent into the front line during a battle and many of them were killed or wounded. Because they were not Roman citizens they were not valued as highly as legionaries.

Another important ▶ job the auxiliaries had was to man the forts and walls that protected the borders of the Empire. This photograph was taken from the top of Hadrian's Wall, which for most of the time was the northernmost point of the Roman Empire. Although built by the legions by order of the Emperor Hadrian in A.D. 122, it was manned by auxiliary troops and acted as a barrier against the troublesome tribes of northern Britain. The wall hugs the hills and crags. It was an amazing engineering feat, joining the east and west coasts of Britain.

A number of forts were built along Hadrian's Wall. At one called Housteads visitors can see an unusual building. It is the toilet block used by the soldiers. The two narrow channels are where the men washed the sponges they used to clean themselves – as we use toilet paper today. The block shows how well organized these forts were. ▶

The many soldiers' tombstones that have been found around the Empire are a great source of information about the army. Because they did not want to be forgotten if they died far away from home, soldiers paid into a fund for a tombstone after their death. The stone in the picture shows a very important rank of soldier – a **centurion** from the 20th legion (one of the legions that built Hadrian's Wall). His armor is shown on the stone. A centurion was in charge of eighty legionaries, often a difficult job. To show his rank he carried a staff, which he often used to hit his unruly legionaries. ▼

TOWN LIFE

Towns were very important in the growth of the Roman Empire. Roman ideas were spread through the hundreds of towns in the Empire that acted as centers of trade, religion, entertainment, and learning. They were also centers of local government, and they provided protection in times of danger. In the towns of the Empire, the local population could see Roman *architecture,* fashion, laws, sports, and *hygiene.* This encouraged them to follow Roman ways.

Romans had very high standards of hygiene, and the ***sewage systems*** in their towns were remarkable. There was a plentiful supply of clean water. Since rivers and streams in towns were often polluted, a clean water spring was found, and an ***aqueduct*** was built, along which the water was carried. The Romans used more water per person than the people in New York City use today. The picture shows part of the aqueduct that supplied water to Nîmes in France. Striding dramatically across a valley, this aqueduct carried pure water from 25 miles away.

Most water was used for washing and ▶ drinking. It was supplied to fountains, and the excess water was used to flush out the drains. More important, the water was used to feed the public baths built near the town forum. Romans liked to bathe daily and were very clean. Bathing often took place after work when people visited the public baths on the way home. The baths were very cheap and the bath houses provided wine, food, and entertainment. The picture shows the Roman baths at Bath in England. Although everything above the bases of the pillars was added in the nineteenth century, it is easy to imagine bathers chatting and drinking on the edge or jumping in.

Bathing houses ◀ were heated by a *furnace* and *hypocaust system*. The hot air from the furnace was channeled into an area under a floor supported by pillars, as shown in the picture. This made the room very hot, so the bathers would sweat before taking their bath. The hypocaust could also heat houses, which was very useful in cold parts of the Empire such as Gaul (present-day France) and Britain. In the picture the air channels are visible at the sides of the walls.

15

We know a lot about Roman towns from the exciting archaeological discoveries at Pompeii and Herculaneum, near Naples in Italy. Both towns were lost after the volcano Vesuvius erupted in A.D. 79, covering the towns in layers of volcanic mud, ash, and lava. For centuries they lay forgotten, until the area was carefully uncovered. The results were amazing: streets, houses, *artifacts*, shops, bakeries, bars, barbers shops, and laundries were preserved exactly as they were on the day the volcano erupted.

▲ At this wine bar, the jars are still perfectly in place. These kept the wine cool. It is easy to imagine a busy lunchtime full of drinkers having a snack of beans or lentils. Pompeii had at least 120 such bars.

◄ Poor people in Roman towns lived in small apartment buildings, but the rich could afford fine stone town houses with tiled roofs, which tend to be better preserved. Many town houses had luxurious rooms, bath suites, mosaic floors, and beautiful gardens. This garden is at a house in Herculaneum.

Because ► archaeologists have found many artifacts they have been able to reconstruct the rooms from which they came. This is a typical town house kitchen. The large storage containers are called amphorae. There is also a large cooking pot and an oven.

COUNTRY LIFE

Our knowledge of the countryside in the Roman Empire is not as complete as our knowledge of the towns. What life was like for peasant farmers and slaves living in outlying settlements is less certain. We do know that farming was very important because enough food had to be produced to feed the huge Roman army and the millions of town and city dwellers. Life was very hard for people in the countryside – they worked all day in the fields, cleared forests, or labored in mines and quarries.

In the Roman Empire good farming land was divided up into estates. Some were owned by rich tribal farmers who had become Roman citizens, while others rented them from landlords. Many estates were owned by the emperor himself. Archaeologists have discovered that at the heart of these estates were large villas. Villa in Latin means farm, so it refers to the farm estates as well as the country home. Looking at the mosaic of a north African estate with the villa at its center, we can guess at some of the activities that took place there.

At one time archaeologists tended to concentrate only on villa buildings, but recently they have learned a lot more about the estates as a whole. Villas were made possible by successful, well-organized farming. The farm profits helped pay for villas that were luxuriously built and extended. This villa was enlarged to include heated rooms, bath suites, and a mosaic-floored dining room.

This mosaic comes ▶ from a country villa in north Africa. A banquet is taking place. The man in the middle is serving food. The guests are being entertained with music while they eat. The man in the bottom right is playing panpipes.

APPEARANCE

We tend to think of all Romans as wearing togas, but the toga was such a complicated piece of clothing that by the time of the Empire, it was mainly worn only for special ceremonies by wealthy citizens. Most poorer people usually wore simple woolen tunics with holes for the arms and head, held in at the waist by a belt.

The men on this carving are wearing togas. Made of wool or silk, the toga had to be three times the length of the wearer and was wrapped around the body leaving the right arm uncovered. During cold weather a heavy woolen cloak was worn over it.

This is a Roman couple. The woman ▶
has ringlets and a hair band. She is holding a
writing pen called a stylus and a writing tablet
made of wax. With the stylus she would cut
letters into a wax "page." Her husband wears
his hair short, although it is also curled. This
was done by a hairdresser with a curling iron.
It was fashionable for men to wear perfume
and face paint. Beards went in and out of
fashion – this man has a faint, wispy beard.

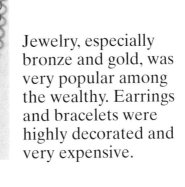

Jewelry, especially
bronze and gold, was
very popular among
the wealthy. Earrings
and bracelets were
highly decorated and
very expensive.

ENTERTAINMENT

Because life was hard in Roman times, people living in the Empire loved entertainment. It was said that the only things Romans were interested in were entertainment and food. If you lived near a town or city there was a very good chance of finding regular entertainment in either the theaters or the *arenas* built in the big settlements. Emperors realized that one way of remaining popular with the people of Rome was to provide free shows. These were known as the Roman Games. Men, often slaves, were specially trained as gladiators to fight to the death in the arena. Other shows included men fighting wild animals, chariot races, animal hunts, and even sea battles (they had to flood the arena)!

◄ The first arena – or amphitheater – was built around 53 B.C. The most famous amphitheater was the Colosseum in Rome, which is shown in the picture. The crowds would have been seated on the raised tiers. Still there, below the level of the floor, are the cells and corridors where the wild animals and gladiators waited until they were called to fight. Above them would have been 50,000 noisy spectators.

▼ One of the most popular spectator sports in the Empire was chariot racing, which is shown in the carving below. The reason for its popularity was its great danger. Teams of charioteers would race at high speed, pushing and bumping each other as they went. One trick was to smash deliberately into the opposing chariots, hoping to destroy them. When this happened, the charioteer was "shipwrecked," and he had to cut the reins quickly or risk being dragged by his own horses to death or serious injury. In Rome these races took place at the Circus Maximus, which could hold 250,000 spectators. By our standards these sports were very violent – most involved humans and animals in acts of great cruelty. However, their popularity shows how brutal and cheap life was in those days.

▲ Gladiators took part in fights against each other and against wild beasts. The Roman audience loved to watch men fighting to the death. Gladiators could not usually expect to live for longer than two or three fights in the arena, although sometimes a defeated man was allowed to live. If a gladiator did manage to win five fights in a row he was rewarded with his freedom.

GODS AND BURIAL

The Romans believed in many gods, and they allowed different kinds of religious worship within their Empire. They drew the line at human sacrifice, and this explains why Druidism – the religion of many *Iron Age* tribes – was brutally crushed by the army. In the main Roman religion, there were three major Roman gods and goddesses: Jupiter, Juno, and Minerva. They had a special temple on the most sacred hill in Rome, the Capitol. Later in Roman history, emperors were also considered gods, usually after their deaths.

◄ The painted statue shows the third most important goddess, Minerva. She was the goddess of wisdom, healing, and arts and crafts.

Worship took place ► not only in temples, but also at home. Many people had *shrines* in their homes to honor the local gods. This late Roman carving in ivory shows a woman making an offering at a shrine.

SYMMACHORVM

▼ The Romans were less tolerant of Christianity, probably because it was such a new religion and was not rooted in Roman tradition. As a result Christians were often treated very cruelly. However, after the Emperor Constantine became a Christian in A.D. 324, Christianity spread to many parts of the Empire. This baptism pool was found in a Roman temple that was converted to an early Christian church in Tunisia.

The Romans also ▶
took in a number of
religions from the
Middle East. One,
called Mithraism, was
a secret and
mysterious religion
practiced only by
men. In a legend, the
god Mithras had to
kill a bull, whose
blood had life-giving
properties. This
religion was very
popular with soldiers,
and a Mithraic
Temple was built
close to Hadrian's
Wall.

◀ Roman law was
very strict concerning
the burial of the dead.
Except for babies,
people could not be
buried in towns and
cities, and *cemeteries*
had to be outside city
boundaries. Rich
people were buried in
tombs. The picture
shows some tombs on
the left. Poor people
were *cremated*, and
their ashes were
either buried or
placed in pots. Some
of these pots stand in
the grass in front of
the tombs.

THE FALL OF ROME

By the third century A.D. tribes outside the Roman Empire began raiding provinces in the hope of taking rich pickings. In response to this threat the boundaries of the Empire were strengthened and some cities built walls or added turrets to existing walls. Around the coasts of Gaul and Britain special forts were built to keep a lookout for Anglo-Saxon raiders, who came in longships from what is now Germany.

The huge towers of this ancient fort helped defenders see along their walls and also improved their fire power. The remains of a defensive ditch are in front of the towers. The ditch would have been much deeper 1,700 years ago.

As the attacks on ▶ the Empire continued, it became very difficult to collect taxes: people either refused or had no money to pay. This meant that the army could not be paid, so many soldiers deserted, leaving the Empire undefended. Once the army left an area, the Roman way of life collapsed remarkably quickly. Buildings were deserted, *pillaged*, burned, or left in ruins. In this picture of a once proud Roman city, people are living in clusters in the ruins. The large ruin in the center was the theater. The city walls are crumbling and unmanned.
(On display in England in the Canterbury Heritage Museum ©.)

▲ By the fifth century A.D. tribes from central Europe – the Franks, Vandals, Goths, and Huns – were making serious inroads into Roman territory. One of these tribes, the Huns, was led by Attila, who appears on this medal. The Romans called these tribes barbarians because they lived outside the Empire and were not "civilized." The writing on the medal calls Attila the "*Scourge* of God."

The Roman ▶
Empire was very
powerful while it was
growing; but defending
the frontier proved to
be too difficult. By
A.D. 476 the Empire
had broken up. This
is the large city wall
that bordered
Constantinople (now
Istanbul in Turkey)
around which the
Eastern Empire was
based. Constantinople
survived until the
fifteenth century, but
the once mighty
Western Empire lay
in ruins.

GLOSSARY

Aqueduct A bridge for carrying water.

Archaeologists People who study objects and remains from the past.

Architecture The design and style of buildings.

Arena A place with seats around an open space where games or contests are held.

Artifacts Objects, such as tools or pots, that archaeologists study to find out how people used to live.

Barbarian The Romans called all tribespeople who lived outside the Empire barbarians. According to the Romans they were "uncivilized," because they did not speak Latin or Greek.

Branded Stamped with a hot iron.

Cemeteries Places where dead people are buried.

Centurion A Roman soldier who was in charge of a group of eighty legionaries (called a century).

Citizens Members of a state or country who must obey its government and laws, and who have certain rights.

Civilian A person who is not in the armed forces.

Cremate To burn a dead body to ashes.

Empire A group of countries or states under one ruler.

Engineers People who design and make buildings, machines, roads, and bridges.

Excavated Dug up buried ruins.

Fertile A word describing land that is good for farming because it is rich in the nutrients that plants need to help them grow.

Furnace A structure, like a very big oven, that can produce great heat.

Hygiene Clean or healthy practices.

Hypocaust system The Romans' way of heating buildings by spreading hot air beneath the floor.

Iron Age The period, which began in about 1100 B.C., when iron began to be used widely.

Legend A story handed down from earlier times.

Mosaic A design made by arranging lots of small pieces of marble, stone, etc.

Pillage To rob from a town during a war.

Scourge A whip; someone or something that causes wide suffering.

Sewage system A system to carry water and waste matter away from buildings.

Shrines Places of worship.

Slavery A system that permits the ownership of slaves.

Slaves People who are owned by and forced to work for other people.

IMPORTANT DATES

B.C.	
c 753	Rome founded
c 507	Roman Republic founded
312	First Roman aqueduct completed
146	Carthage destroyed. Romans control the Mediterranean Sea
51	Gaul (mainly France) becomes part of the Roman Empire
27	Augustus becomes the first Roman Emperor
4?	Birth of Jesus Christ

A.D.	
43	Britain invaded and conquered
79	Eruption of Vesuvius – Pompeii and Herculaneum destroyed
113	Trajan's Column built
122	Hadrian's Wall in Britain built
293	Roman Empire split into east and west under two emperors
323	Emperor Constantine becomes a Christian
360	Picts (ancient people of north Britain) and Scots cross Hadrian's Wall
455	Vandals sack Rome
476	Western Roman Empire destroyed

BOOKS TO READ

Bombarde, Odile and Moatti, Claude. *Living in Ancient Rome*. Ossining, NY: Young Discovery Library, 1988.

Corbishley, Mike. *The Romans*. History as Evidence. New York: Warwick Press, 1984.

Corbishley, Mike. *What Do We Know About the Romans?*. New York: Peter Bedrick Books, 1992.

Dillon, Eilis. *Living in Imperial Rome*. Chester Springs, PA: Dufour Editions, 1991.

Ganeri, Anita. *Romans*. Focus On. New York: Gloucester Press, 1992.

Mulvihill, Margaret. *Roman Forts*. History Highlights. New York: Gloucester Press, 1990.

Usher, Kerry. *Heroes, Gods and Emperors from Roman Mythology*. New York: Peter Bedrick Books, 1992.

INDEX